Christmas EVERGREENS

TIMELESS PIANO ARRANGEMENTS OF CLASSIC CAROLS

GlorySound

A Division of Shawnee Press, Inc.
1221 17th Ave. South, Nashville, TN 37212

VISIT SHAWNEE PRESS ONLINE AT WWW.SHAWNEEPRESS.COM

JOY TO THE WORLD

ANTIOCH
George Frideric Handel
Arranged by MARK HAYES

Moderately fast (♩ = ca. 108 - 112)

for Mary and Mark Patterson

Canon de Noël

Canon and Gigue
by Johann Pachelbel (c.1653-1706) &
The First Nowell,
English Carol, Sandys' *Christmas Carols,* 1833

Arranged by
JOSEPH M. MARTIN (BMI)

Ukrainian Bell Carol

Arranged by SHIRLEY BRENDLINGER

MYKOLA LEONTOVICH
(1877-1921)

ANGELS WE HAVE HEARD ON HIGH

Traditional French Carol
Arranged by CINDY BERRY

What Child Is This?

Arranged by SHIRLEY BRENDLINGER

ENGLISH MELODY

Copyright © 2001, GlorySound
A Division of Shawnee Press, Inc.

2nd time to Coda, p. 22

Come, Thou Long-Expected Jesus

Rowland H. Prichard (1811-1887)
Arranged by Chuck Marohnic

21

RISE UP, SHEPHERDS, AND FOLLOW

Negro Spiritual
Arranged by MARK HAYES

for Scott Gyer

Prelude on "Adeste Fideles"

Arranged by MICHAEL COX

Music by JOHN FRANCIS WADE

28

for Andrew and Rebecca

Children, Go Where I Send Thee/
Go, Tell It on the Mountain

African-American Spirituals

Arranged by
JOSEPH M. MARTIN (BMI)

Copyright © 1997, Malcolm Music
A Division of Shawnee Press, Inc.
International Copyright Secured   All Rights Reserved
SOLE SELLING AGENT: SHAWNEE PRESS, INC., NASHVILLE, TN 37212

Moderately slow gospel blues ($\quarternote$ = ca. 66)

Infant Holy

with

He Is Born, the Divine Christ Child

Arranged by
BRANT ADAMS (BMI)

Tune: W ZLOBIE LEZY
Traditional Polish carol
Tune: IL EST NE´
Traditional French carol

Happily, lightly flowing (♩. = *ca*.66)

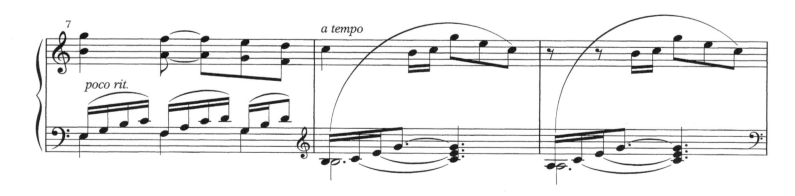

O Come, O Come, Emmanuel

(VENI EMMANUEL)

Arranged by
LLOYD LARSON
Adapted from Plainsong
Thomas Helmore

52

The Friendly Beasts

Medieval French Carol
Arranged by Chuck Marohnic

for Sue and Richard Beal

Away in a Manger

Tune: *Mueller*
James R. Murray (1841-1905)
Arranged by
JOSEPH M. MARTIN (BMI)

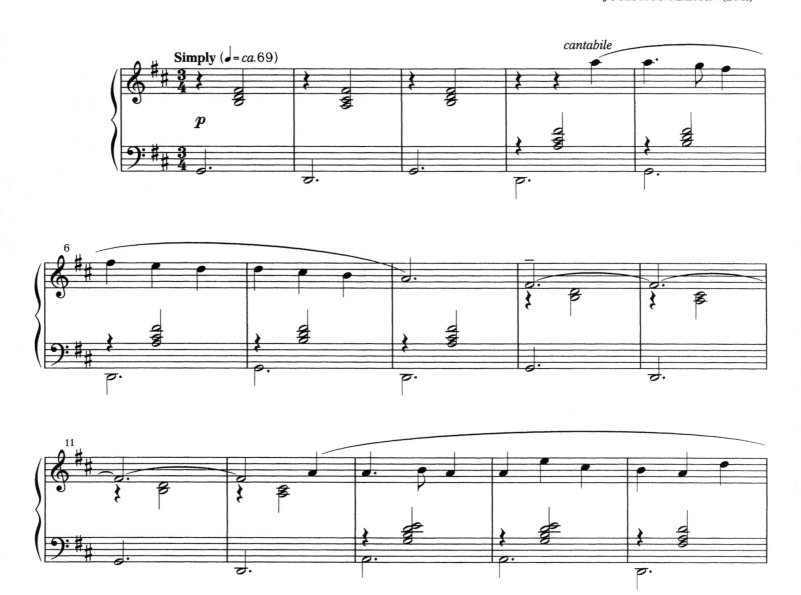

58

O Little Town of Bethlehem

FOREST GREEN (Traditional English melody)
Arranged by LLOYD LARSON (ASCAP)

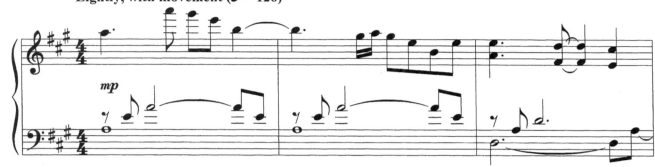

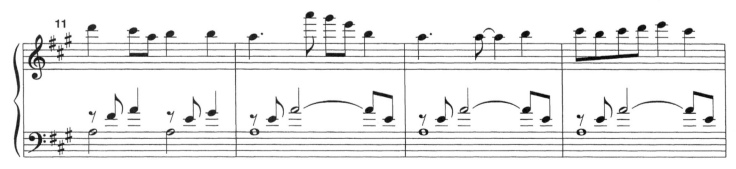

to Don and Mary Brock

Of the Father's Love Begotten

Arranged by LARRY SHACKLEY (ASCAP)

Melody: Thirteenth-century Plainsong

LONELY MIDNIGHT

Arranged by JAMES M. STEVENS

JIMBO STEVENS

With a quiet serenity ($\quarternote$ = ca. 58)

O HOW JOYFULLY

Arranged by
VICKI TUCKER COURTNEY (ASCAP)

O SANCTISSIMA
Traditional Italian Tune